A Parent's Guide to Teen FOMO

A Parent's Guide to Influencers

A Parent's Guide to Instagram

A Parent's Guide to TikTok

A Parent's Guide to YouTube

A Parent's Guide to Teen Identity

A Parent's Guide to LGBTQ+ & Your Teen

A Parent's Guide to Body Positivity

A Parent's Guide to Eating Disorders

A Parent's Guide to Fear & Worry

A PARENT'S GUIDE TO TEEN IDENTITY

A PARENT'S GUIDE TO

TEEN
IDENTITY

axis

Tyndale House Publishers
Carol Stream, Illinois

For information about special discounts for bulk purchases, please contact Tyndale House Publishers at csresponse@tyndale.com, or call 1-855-277-9400.

Library of Congress Cataloging-in-Publication Data

A catalog record for this book is available from the Library of Congress.

ISBN 978-1-4964-6734-8

Printed in the United States of America

29	28	27	26	25	24	23
7	6	5	4	3	2	1

The secret of my identity is hidden in the love and mercy of God.... Therefore I cannot hope to find myself anywhere except in Him.... Therefore there is only one problem on which all my existence, my peace and my happiness depend: to discover myself in discovering God. If I find Him I will find myself and if I find my true self I will find Him.

THOMAS MERTON, *NEW SEEDS OF CONTEMPLATION*

CONTENTS

A LETTER FROM AXIS

Dear Reader,

We're Axis, and since 2007, we've been creating resources to help connect parents, teens, and Jesus in a disconnected world. We're a group of gospel-minded researchers, speakers, and content creators, and we're excited to bring you the best of what we've learned about making meaningful connections with the teens in your life.

This parent's guide is designed to help start a conversation. Our goal is to give you enough knowledge that you're able to ask your teen informed questions about their world. For each guide, we spend weeks reading, researching, and interviewing parents and teens in order to distill everything you need to know about the topic at hand. We encourage you to read the whole thing and then to use the questions we include to get the conversation going with your teen—and then to follow the conversation wherever it leads.

As Douglas Stone, Bruce Patton, and Sheila Heen point out in their book *Difficult Conversations*, "Changes in attitudes and behavior rarely come about because of arguments, facts, and attempts to persuade. How often do *you* change your values and beliefs—or whom you love or what you want in life—based on something someone tells you? And how likely are you to do so when the person who is trying to change you doesn't seem fully aware of the reasons you see things differently in the first place?"[1] For whatever reason, when we believe that others are trying to understand *our* point of view, our defenses usually go down, and we're more willing to listen to *their* point of view. The rising generation is no exception.

So we encourage you to ask questions, to listen, and then to share your heart with your teen. As we often say at Axis, discipleship happens where conversation happens.

Sincerely,
Your friends at Axis

---

[1] Douglas Stone, Bruce Patton, and Sheila Heen, *Difficult Conversations: How to Discuss What Matters Most*, rev. ed. (New York: Penguin Books, 2010), 137.

WHY IS IDENTITY SUCH A BIG DEAL?

IN THE HEART OF EVERY PERSON is a deep-rooted question: "Who am I, and how do I fit into the world around me?" In other words, what makes me "me"? Am I the roles that I play (friend, sibling, athlete)? Am I a set of characteristics (quiet, bubbly, confident)? Am I my thoughts, emotions, body, soul, actions . . . a summation of these things?

The question of identity shows up in which brands teens choose to wear, in how they manage their appearance with friends, in their desire to get good grades or try out for sports or musicals, and in what they think about themselves and others while scrolling through social media.[1]

It can be difficult to navigate our teens' search for identity with healthy language, perspective, and grace. The Christian story for the world has a stunning message about who we are. Our challenge is to contextualize that story in the modern world, the world of popular culture.

The question of identity shows up in which brands teens choose to wear, in how they manage their appearance with friends, in their desire to get good grades or try out for sports or musicals, and in what they think about themselves and others while scrolling through social media.

WHAT DOES CULTURE SAY ABOUT IDENTITY?

MODERN WESTERN CULTURE PRESENTS new challenges for identity formation. Identity used to be bestowed, not created or discovered. Two hundred years ago, if your father was a farmer, it was assumed that you would also be a farmer. Identity wasn't about personal feelings or dreams. Instead, the cultural ideal was that people would sacrifice individual desires for the good of the community.

Today's American culture bristles at the idea of an authority figure telling us who we should be or what we should do. Culture tells us that we must look inside to our desires and intuitions to discover who we are. "Follow your heart," even if your family or society disagrees with what you choose. Self-expression is often considered the highest value.

In his sermon "Being the Beloved," Henri Nouwen said every person is tempted to ground their identity in three lies:

1. "I am what I have."

2. "I am what I do."

3. "I am what other people say or think of me."[2]

Having wealth or material success, doing important work, and being admired can all be things we look to in order to gain a sense of identity. The first two lies are especially relevant to teens who are under intense pressure to maximize every spare moment for college applications. They may learn to identify themselves primarily by their accomplishments, whether as athletes, artists, or honor students. The

Having wealth or material success, doing important work, and being admired can all be things we look to in order to gain a sense of identity.

temptation to build an identity around success can endure for a lifetime.

And in a world of online personas and cancel culture,[3] lie #3 is maybe more persuasive than it's ever been. We get to decide which pictures to post, whom to follow, and what information to include or leave out. With screens between us and time to edit ourselves, we have the ability to totally remake our image—which comes with the pressure to do it perfectly.

WHERE DOES GEN Z GET ITS IDENTITY FROM?

GEN Z IS KNOWN AS THE "ALWAYS ON" generation.[4] It's a fitting label. At any moment, your teen could appear on someone's Snap story or in the background of a friend's TikTok video. In a way, they're always on display, which can result in a pressure to curate and present and edit their best selves all the time. In much of today's culture, the average person's sense of identity is only as stable as the number of likes on their most recent post.

Traditional aspects of identity such as occupation, education level, or location are still very important for many teens, but they're less formative for Gen Z than they were for previous generations.[5] They can find like-minded community virtually, so they aren't confined to the belief systems or values of the people around them.

There are probably many ways that your teen deviates from the average Gen Zer, but this is what researchers have observed about Gen Z's behavior so far:

Identity is self-determined and individualistic: Gen Z sees "experiences, hobbies, likes and dislikes, and social circle as most crucial to defining themselves."[6] Which is why they might add a fourth lie to Nouwen's list: "I am who I decide to be." They strongly believe in a world where self-expression, uniqueness, and difference are welcome.

> *"What I choose to enjoy and pursue (jobs, education, relationship) plays a lot more heavily on my life than where I'm from or my heritage."*
> —20-year-old[7]

"I converted to Islam when I was 14, which dramatically altered my lifestyle and social milieu." —23-year-old[8]

"I'm bisexual and also from a conservative Christian family. Although I'm gay and liberal, I'm constantly surrounded by Republicans." —21-year-old[9]

Identity is ongoing and fluid: Teens are on a never-ending quest to curate their best and most authentic self. In one survey, most Gen Zers strongly agreed that "identity is a work in progress— expressed by what you're putting out into the world and how others are responding to it."[10]

"Identity is something that can change, like politics. That's a belief

shared by a lot of my generation."
—17-year-old[11]

Inclusivity is a must: Gen Z is the most racially diverse generation; 72 percent believe racial equality is the most important current issue. Inclusivity extends to gender as well. Twenty-seven percent of teens identified as nonbinary in a California survey.[12]

> *"We think in terms of we. When I go to the polls . . . I'm not just thinking about the people who live on my street. I'm thinking about the people who I'm connected to on social media from all around the world and thinking about how my vote and my life affect them. And I think that that ethos is a core tenet of our generation." —19-year-old[13]*

Meaning-oriented: Ninety-five percent of teens surveyed by the Pew Research Center said that having a fulfilling job is very important. Eighty-one percent said that helping others is very important. By comparison, getting married and having children are much lower priorities to Gen Z.[14]

> *"I'm going to school for a degree*
> *I know won't get me a job but*
> *I would rather be in debt and*
> *producing important cultural work*
> *than financially stable and leading*
> *an uninteresting life."*
> —23-year-old[15]

Justice-oriented: Eighty percent of teens support Black Lives Matter, 74 percent support transgender rights, and 63 percent support feminism.[16]

Stressed and sad: According to Pew Research Center, "The total number of teenagers who recently experienced depression increased 59% between 2007 and 2017." Seven of ten American teens believe that depression and anxiety are noteworthy problems for themselves and their peers and cite academic and social pressures as the most common causes.[17]

The online self: Teens average three hours per day on social media, a space that they believe gives them more confidence and freedom to be who they really are.[18]

"I am the most confident I can be online and portray a very strong persona when in real life I'm not always 100% able to in my current environment." —23-year-old[19]

"I am who I decide to be."
[Teens] strongly believe
in a world where self-
expression, uniqueness, and
difference are welcome.

"I have few friends [in real life], but I have many close friends online that I talk to and text all of the time. I also have a pen pal I crush on who's from Japan!" —19-year-old[20]

Yet they would still say there's a gap between their most authentic selves and their online representations of self.[21]

CAN THESE THINGS GIVE GEN Z A REAL SENSE OF SELF?

AT FIRST, REMAKING OUR IDENTITY—online or in person—sounds like freedom. Influencers create online profiles worth millions, and much of the appeal for Gen Z is their "authenticity." Yet the thrill teens experience when they see a post go viral is often followed by the pressure to repeat that success, and the fear that they will lose the influence they've worked so hard to gain.

Creating or discovering ourselves can leave us feeling lost, unsure about what to place our identity in. Tim Keller lays out several reasons why a self-referential identity very quickly becomes unlivable. These include

1. It's unstable. Our deepest wants are often contradictory. (I want to be in a committed relationship, and I also want a demanding career. I want to enjoy lots of free time, but

I also want to be productive. I want to look fit and attractive, but I also love French fries. Having all of this at once is impossible.) How do we know which feelings are "us" and which feelings to reject?

2. It's crushing. We not only have to know what we're passionate about, but we also have to *achieve* our dreams if we're going to prove our status and worthiness. When identity is all about achievement, criticism is crushing.[22]

Working for worthiness becomes just another thing that can enslave our teens because the moment they do poorly (in any area—school, social life, online) their whole identity is threatened. This drives Gen Z's fear of being invalidated or "canceled." When identity is performative and measurable, what are we to do with failure? What do we do with the aspects of ourselves that we're ashamed of but that we don't know how to fix?

At first, remaking our identity—online or in person—sounds like freedom. Influencers create online profiles worth millions, and much of the appeal for Gen Z is their "authenticity."

SO WHERE DOES OUR REAL IDENTITY COME FROM?

THE GOSPEL IS SUCH GOOD NEWS for Gen Z because Christ offers an unthreatenable identity that can't be invalidated by mistakes.

We are God's children. One of the most beautiful analogies for the Christian understanding of how we relate to God is that He is our Father and we are His kids. Look at how God the Father and God the Son relate to one another: Jesus lived in obscurity for thirty years, without performing any miracles that we know of, without traveling very far or doing anything particularly noteworthy. As His three years of ministry began, God proclaimed, "This is My beloved Son, in whom I am well pleased."[23] God's favor was already His. Without trying. And God says the same about each of us. We are His beloved children, no matter what we do or fail to do.

We are profoundly loved. When our teens see themselves as God's children, they are invited into an unchanging love. No family drama, no failure at school, no sin struggle, no tragedy can ever change God's love for them.

This identity is received. During an interview with Carey Nieuwhof, Tim Keller explains that Christian identity is the only identity that is received, not achieved. Jesus lost His glory, power, and privilege to pay the penalty for our inhumanity to God and each other, and His life and sacrifice are accessible to everyone. This identity is so secure because it has nothing to do with our performance and everything to do with how Jesus "performed" on our behalf. Knowing full well that we would continue to wound each other, knowing that even with the best

"The gospel is this: We are more sinful and flawed in ourselves than we ever dared believe, yet at the very same time we are more loved and accepted in Jesus Christ than we ever dared hope."

—TIM KELLER

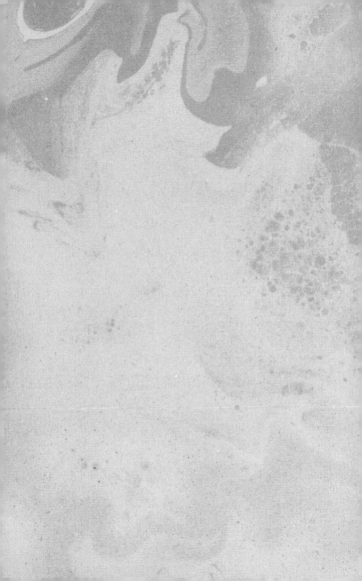

of intentions we would continue to get it wrong, God became a person (what a wild thing to say), and He walked the way that we were always supposed to walk. When we claim Christ's righteousness, we're literally saying that God sees Jesus' perfect obedience when He looks at us.[24]

This identity is redemptive. In our culture, those who aren't open minded, justice oriented, and empathetic are often "canceled," permanently excluded from the table of discussion. We take pride in despising bigots because this often bolsters our own sense of moral superiority. Christian identity doesn't do this. Christian identity says about every person, "You're a sinner. You would be lost without Christ." Yet every person is made in the image of the same God, so we are all equally glorious, equally noble, and even regal. Tim Keller puts it this way: "The gospel is this: We are more sinful and flawed in ourselves than we ever dared believe, yet at the very same time we are more loved and accepted in Jesus Christ than we ever dared hope."[25]

SHOULD WE ALL LOOK THE SAME?

GOD USED HIMSELF AS A TEMPLATE when He created people. So when we love, we reflect God's relational nature; when we create beautiful things, we show off God's artisanship; when we are merciful, we reflect God's mercy.

So will we all end up looking the same since we're all made in the image of the same God? Thankfully, no. We reflect God's image best by becoming more fully ourselves, not by looking like everyone else. *Sanctification* means that we are gradually restored to who we were originally intended to be, not gradually crushed into uniformity. The "body of Christ" is made up of many distinct parts—and that's on purpose.[26]

God is so vast and mysterious and complex that it takes billions of people, thousands of languages, and countless cultures to even start to get a glimpse of everything He is. For instance, Dutch culture is known for its precision, dedication, and thriftiness; these attributes reflect how God is not chaotic but ordered, trustworthy, and steady. And then we find colorful, exuberant, flamboyant cultures in Spain and Portugal and are reminded that God also loves life, that He is emotional, playful, and romantic. Because God is infinite, we'll just keep discovering His depths and mystery.

Being made in the image of God is so profound because by interacting with one another—and even learning more about ourselves—we learn more about who God is. For better or worse, people develop a picture of what God is like when they interact with us.

This is why, in the midst of sharing a common humanity (and bearing the image of the same God), there are still so many differences among the people of the world:

- **Race:** The ways we are physically different from each other, including different skin tones and hair textures. Rooted in biology.

- **Ethnicity:** The unique cultures we come from and all the ways we express values and traditions.

- **Heritage:** The people who have gone before us and contribute to who we become.

- **Maleness and femaleness:** At a chemical and hormonal level, men and women have unique ways of reflecting the image of God.

- **Personality:** Things like introversion and extroversion. These traits impact the way we spend our time, what we crave, and how we relate to the people around us.

These differences are God's gifts to us. Each person we come in contact with reflects a slice of God's nature that we might not experience in anyone else.

Being made in the image of God is so profound because by interacting with one another—and even learning more about ourselves—we learn more about who God is.

WHAT IS THE "FALSE SELF"?

"Inside of me there are two dogs. One is mean and evil and the other is good, and they fight each other all the time. When asked which one wins, I answer, the one I feed the most."

ATTRIBUTED TO SITTING BULL

This quote perfectly describes the battle between the false self and the true self. Even after we are given a completely new life through Jesus, our old identities and ways of seeing the world cling to us. The way I want to be in the world and my actual self are often in conflict. As the apostle Paul writes in Romans 7:17-25,

> If I know the law but still can't keep it, and if the power of sin within me keeps sabotaging my best intentions, I obviously need help! . . . I decide to do good, but

I don't *really* do it; I decide not to do bad, but then I do it anyway. My decisions, such as they are, don't result in actions. Something has gone wrong deep within me and gets the better of me every time.

It happens so regularly that it's predictable. The moment I decide to do good, sin is there to trip me up. I truly delight in God's commands, but it's pretty obvious that not all of me joins in that delight. Parts of me covertly rebel, and just when I least expect it, they take charge. . . .

Is there no one who can do anything for me? Isn't that the real question?

The answer, thank God, is that Jesus Christ can and does. He acted to set things right in this life

of contradictions where I want
to serve God with all my heart
and mind, but am pulled by the
influence of sin to do something
totally different (MSG).

The apostle Paul's solution involved a careful delineation between the desires within us and the real "us," i.e., the part of us that watches and mediates among our desires. When we identify with our thoughts, feelings, and urges, we may assume that they are the truth—and may obey them much more easily.

Colossians 3:3-4 says, "For you died, and your life is now hidden with Christ in God. When Christ, who is your life, appears, then you also will appear with him in glory." My life is hidden with God. Who I really am has nothing to do with my urges, my actions, or my thoughts.

That sounds crazy, but the reality of our new selves being hidden in Christ is that we are already perfect. We are the righteousness of Christ—currently, as we speak. However, our earthly lives have yet to catch up to our eternal reality. God sees us as we can be, but loves us as we are.

Our daily experience can leave us feeling sick of ourselves, despairing that we will never be the kinds of people we know we were created to be. As we fight to see ourselves through God's loving gaze, here's a wonderful encouragement from C. S. Lewis:

> The great thing to remember is that, though our feelings come and go, His love for us does not. It is not wearied by our sins, or our indifference; and, therefore, it is

quite relentless in its determination that we shall be cured of those sins, at whatever cost to us, at whatever cost to Him.[27]

God sees us as we can be,
but loves us as we are.

WHAT ABOUT SELF-KNOWLEDGE?

IF YOU'RE WONDERING, *Is it helpful to sit around and think about myself? Isn't our goal to love God and people, not to know a lot about the self?,* consider this thought from John Calvin:

> Our wisdom, in so far as it ought to be deemed true and solid wisdom, consists almost entirely of two parts: the knowledge of God and of ourselves. But as these are connected together by many ties, it is not easy to determine which of the two precedes, and gives birth to the other.[28]

In his book *Emotionally Healthy Spirituality*, Peter Scazzero explains that our identity includes several components: emotional, social, physical, intellectual, and spiritual. God intends for us to be whole, to not leave any parts of ourselves behind. Your entire being was God's idea; self-awareness is His gift. It allows us to examine our motivations ("Why do I get angry when my teen stays in their room all evening?"), the ways we tend to hurt those we love, helpful and unhelpful communication styles, and even our desires (what we want the most).[29]

We can't grow if we're not aware of weakness, which is why self-discovery tools can be so helpful. These include StrengthsQuest, Myers-Briggs, the Enneagram, True Colors, Four Animals, spiritual gifts tests . . . the list could go on. As your teen goes on a quest to discover who they are, God will be there with them. As they learn about themselves, they will learn about their Creator, and vice versa.

In addition to specific personality tests, we learn about ourselves through community. Your teen needs your input and perspective as they figure themselves out. And you need them, too. Because what we say we value and how we actually behave are often quite different. For instance, someone might say they love hiking, but a friend could point out that they hardly ever get outside. So their self-perception (a lover of hiking) conflicts with what's observable to others. Psychologists have a helpful tool called the Johari window model, which explains that self-knowledge can come from a variety of places.[30] Essentially, there are four quadrants:

Open Self: what we know about ourselves and are willing to share with others

Blind Spot: what we don't know about ourselves but other people notice

Hidden Self: what we know about ourselves but are unwilling to share

Unknown Self: what no one knows about us (neither ourselves nor others)

Confession brings healing, and our wounds are cared for by the people who love us. If no one knows that you are wounded, they cannot love you well. This is the basis for all self-disclosure: being mature enough to ask for what we need instead of assuming that our friends and family will read our minds or know exactly what we crave. Your teen is learning how to do this, and they learn best by watching you.

WHAT IF MY TEEN IS OBSESSED WITH HOW THEY LOOK?

GROWING UP IN THE AGE of social media and selfies, Gen Z obsesses more over their appearance than previous generations.[31] Sure, it sounds a bit narcissistic, but the reasons are more complex than one might expect. Teens know they can be photographed anytime, anywhere, and they expect those images to end up online. Teens view their personal identity as a curated composition; they are building their own personal brand over time. Teens have fun experimenting with their individuality through makeup, hairstyles, and fashion—and sharing that process with their friends.

It can be easy to jump to extremes in this conversation, either by overemphasizing or underemphasizing the importance of image. The truth is that how we represent ourselves matters, but it isn't the truest or most important thing about us.

Taking lots of selfies or watching makeup tutorials isn't necessarily a sign of narcissism. Part of discovering who we are is discovering who we're not; your teen may "try on" a few images that might seem a little weird to you. Unless there are clear warning signs (like posts about self-harm), it's usually best not to take this experimentation too seriously.

A friend of ours bleached his hair in high school, and although his dad reacted very critically, his grandma laughed with him about it and didn't judge him. This was one of several interactions that helped him to see her as "safe." Over time she became one of the most important spiritual mentors in his life.

Of course, it's one thing if you explicitly told your teen that they aren't allowed to get tattoos, piercings, or dye their hair, and then they do it anyway. It's completely different if you haven't communicated any explicit rules about these things, and they do one of them. Nagging them about it on the back end can leave our teens feeling unsupported and insecure.

We can actually push teens toward an *unhealthy* view of image when we comment too regularly about their appearance. Sometimes the impulse to do so comes from a fear that others will look at how our teen acts or dresses and make judgment calls about our parenting. What looks like concern about our teen's image may actually be concern about our own.

Teens view their personal identity as a curated composition; they are building their own personal brand over time.

HOW CAN WE LIVE OUT OUR REAL IDENTITIES?

"PUT YOUR IDENTITY IN CHRIST." We've all heard the cheesy sermons about resisting peer pressure and believing we're beautiful because we're God's kids. But when your daughter's boyfriend just broke up with her, or your son was just told to go kill himself by another gamer, this Christian cliché (even though it's true!) may not feel great. Unfortunately, there's not a formula for seeing ourselves the way God sees us—which is tough, but also probably a good thing because it means we can't ride along on each other's coattails. We have to ask Christ what He thinks of us for ourselves; no one else can do that for your teen. Here are some practical ways for your teen to begin to root their identity in Christ.

Let some relationships go. How do our teens know if a friend is helping or hurting them? Probably through some reflection on the relationship. Ask them questions like these: "How do you feel when you're around this friend?" "Which friends allow you to feel comfortable as your full self?" "Do you have any friends that require you to change when you're with them?"

Be generous and give something away. Our old nature is utterly self-centered. By parting with something we like, we're reminding our flesh that our identity is not rooted in what we possess—and that our new nature in Christ gets to have the final word in how we behave.

Limit social media. If your teen feels more anxious or depressed after spending lots of time on social media, that's a good sign to either take a break or set some boundaries (i.e., "I won't look at Instagram at night because that's when I feel bored, lonely, and like my life isn't as glamorous as it should be").

Take a moment to be present. Charlotte Markay, a researcher and psychology expert, explains that teens sometimes become so obsessed with image and appearance that "they are living for what they will post later, as opposed to posting what they have already lived."[32] Leave your phones behind for a day. Experience a moment together without taking pictures.

Find vulnerable community. We should all have at least one person who knows everything about us—the good, the bad, and the ugly. Does your teen have a space where they are fully seen and still loved?

Read Scripture. A simple way for students to study the Bible is to ask three questions as they read:

1. What does this passage say about God?

2. What does this passage say about myself?

3. Today, how should I think, act, and feel?[33]

Talk to God. Encourage your teens to ask the Lord, "How do You see me?" "In what ways am I uniquely made in Your image?" "What areas of my life am I holding back from You?" Invite them to speak this over their identity: "I am Your beloved child, and You are well pleased with me."

Identify false beliefs and transform them. Cognitive behavioral therapy is based on the reality that our thoughts, feelings, and actions are interrelated. By changing what we think (or what we do), we can actually change how we feel! The process looks like this:

We have to ask Christ what He thinks of us for ourselves; no one else can do that for your teen.

1. Identify the negative emotion:
   "I feel embarrassed, inadequate,
   discouraged, etc."

2. Identify the unhealthy thought that
   created this emotion: "I failed my
   math test."

3. Identify the lie: "People won't like
   me if I make mistakes—my worth
   depends on my intelligence."

4. Identify the truth: "What does God
   have to say in Scripture about who
   I really am?" In this case, Ephesians
   1:7-10 is a good starting place.

5. Truth summary: "I failed my
   math test. Yet my identity is not
   grounded in success or failure;
   instead, it is grounded in the
   person of Christ. Because of Jesus,
   I am enough."[34]

Define success differently: Researchers have "observed a notable shift away from internal, or intrinsic goals, which one can control, toward extrinsic ones, which are set by the world, and which are increasingly unforgiving."[35] When life doesn't go quite according to plan, how will your teen respond? If our focus shifted from measurable outcomes that we don't have much control over (relationship status, number of followers) to the type of people we want to become, we might feel much happier.

These practices are small steps toward full surrender to God. As Stanley Hauerwas put it, "Christianity is not a set of beliefs or doctrines you believe in order to be a Christian, but rather Christianity is to have one's body shaped, one's habits determined, in a manner that the worship of God is unavoidable."[36]

FINAL THOUGHTS

WHEN THE APOSTLE JOHN writes about himself in his Gospel account, he calls himself "the disciple whom Jesus loved."[37] That's a bold claim; honestly, it sounds arrogant. Is he saying he was closer to Jesus than the other disciples were? Claiming to be more favored or wanted than the rest?

Or perhaps he is claiming the truest thing about his identity. His deepest self was rooted in Christ's love. It was his title, the main thing he wanted to communicate about himself. Interestingly, Jesus also rooted His identity in His belovedness. He is the fullest and best expression of humanity. He is making us more and more like Him—and someday, in our perfection, we will be as fully human as He is. This will mean a lot of things, but it will especially mean that we will love the way God loves: the world, others, and yes, even ourselves. Hmm, self-love? Isn't that mystical and verging on self-worship? Perhaps it's more about humble and honest self-acceptance:

> This closeness with Jesus chips away at our self-pity and shame, forming true humility within us. We take ownership of our mistakes, but don't let them own us; we celebrate our accomplishments, knowing they were accomplished by God's grace. It's a humility that says, "God, you did a good job when you created me and recreated me. Thank you!"[38]

You are God's idea. God dreamed you up . . . with all of your personality quirks and idiosyncrasies. And Christ has nothing but love for you. Every part of you. Of course, because He loves us, He rescues us from destructive habits and thought patterns. Yet even now, while we are not yet perfect, He enjoys us. Perhaps this is why Jesus was able to love so well—He knew that He was fully accepted by the Father, with nothing to prove and nothing to lose. He didn't have to measure up or grasp for worthiness. So He lived in compassion instead of criticism, in perfect security. This is what we want for our teens. For them to see themselves as God sees them: co-heirs with Christ.[39] Righteous.[40] Wonderfully made.[41] Then they will be able to see others (and the world) with God's loving gaze.

You are God's idea. God dreamed you up ... with all of your personality quirks and idiosyncrasies. And Christ has nothing but love for you. Every part of you.

RECAP

- Teens' search for identity is nothing new; it is inside of every human.

- Image and identity are not the same thing. While image (how we appear in the eyes of others) is important, identity is who we really are.

- Identity cannot be rooted in what we do, what we have, or what people say about us because these things are fading.[42] Identity goes far deeper than our accomplishments, talents, possessions, reputation, or relationships.

- Being made in God's image gives us value and purpose.

- In Christ, we are God's children, making us supremely loved and accepted.

- Living into our real identity requires putting off our false identity.

PERSONAL REFLECTION QUESTIONS

1. Is my identity, or sense of self-worth, tied to how my kids behave or appear? Do I believe that my value comes from having a beautiful and put-together family?

2. What do my kids do that embarrasses me? Why are those behaviors or actions embarrassing? Are they actually reflections on my parenting?

3. How is my teen unique? Do I make space for them to fully express the ways they reflect God's image?

4. How do I allow God to speak to my identity? How can I share my identity struggles and growth with my teen?

DISCUSSION QUESTIONS

1. How would you answer the question "Who are you?"

2. What do you want other people to see when they look at you?

3. What feelings do you get when you think about God as your Father?

4. How does God's unchanging love for you affect how you think about who you are?

5. What are some practical and personal ways for you to connect with your Creator and live into your real identity?

6. How have you begun to experience your own uniqueness in the context of helping others?

7. What keeps you from seeing yourself as God sees you?

8. What does authenticity look like?

9. What does an authentic community look like?

10. What does it mean to follow in the way of Jesus today, no matter what success or failure you may experience?

SOCIAL MEDIA DISCUSSION QUESTIONS

1. What makes you want to share a picture or video? What kind of feedback do you hope to get when you post something?

2. Do you follow anyone who makes you feel inadequate? What about their profile makes you feel insecure?

3. Do you follow anyone who encourages you?

4. How does social media impact your self-worth and identity?

ADDITIONAL RESOURCES

1. Eric Geigler, *Identity: Who You Are in Christ*

2. Rankin Wilbourne, *Union with Christ*

3. Jaquelle Crowe, *This Changes Everything*

4. Henri Nouwen, *Life of the Beloved*

5. Peter Scazzero, *Emotionally Healthy Spirituality*

6. Christopher L. Huertz, *The Sacred Enneagram*

7. Tim Keller, "Our Identity: The Christian Alternative to Late Modernity's Story," https://www.youtube.com/watch?v=Ehw87PqTwKw

NOTES

1. "ExpressVPN Survey Reveals the Extent of Gen Z's Social Media Fixation," ExpressVPN, December 1, 2021, https://www.expressvpn .com/blog/gen-z-social-media-survey/.

2. Henri Nouwen, "Being the Beloved," sermon, Crystal Cathedral, 1992, video, 17:58, https:// www.youtube.com/watch?v=v8U4V4aaNWk.

3. "Online Shaming," Wikipedia, accessed May 30, 2022, https://en.wikipedia.org/wiki/Online _shaming.

4. "Is Real Estate Ready for Generation Z?," Dotloop, accessed May 30, 2022, https://www .dotloop.com/blog/generation-z-in-real-estate/.

5. Ben Wiedmaier, "Gen Z, Identity, and Brand: How the 'Digital Native' Generation Is Designing Itself," People Nerds, dscout, accessed May 30, 2022, https://dscout.com /people-nerds/gen-z-identity.

6. Wiedmaier, "Gen Z, Identity, and Brand."

7. Wiedmaier, "Gen Z, Identity, and Brand."

8. Adriana Ramic et al., "900 Voices from Gen Z, America's Most Diverse Generation," *New York Times*, March 22, 2019, https://www .nytimes.com/interactive/2019/us/generation -z.html.

9. Ramic et al., "900 Voices from Gen Z."

10. Wiedmaier, "Gen Z, Identity, and Brand."

11. Dan Levin, "Generation Z: Who They Are, in Their Own Words," *New York Times*, March 28, 2019, https://www.nytimes.com/2019 /03/28/us/gen-z-in-their-words.html.

12. Fisher Phillips, "Move Over, Millennials: Generation Z Comes to the Workplace," Lexology, October 1, 2019, https://www .lexology.com/library/detail.aspx?g=cb59711e -1531-49c4-b4ca-2665afebc97f.

13. Barbara Herman, "Generation Z: Nonrebels with a Cause," R/GA, February 10, 2021, https://www.rga.com/futurevision/trends /generation-z-nonrebels-with-a-cause.

14. Juliana Menasce Horowitz and Nikki Graf, "Most U.S. Teens See Anxiety and Depression as a Major Problem among Their Peers," Pew

Research Center, February 20, 2019, https://
www.pewresearch.org/social-trends/2019
/02/20/most-u-s-teens-see-anxiety-and
-depression-as-a-major-problem-among
-their-peers/.

15. Ramic et al., "900 Voices from Gen Z."

16. Herman, "Generation Z: Nonrebels with
    a Cause."

17. A. W. Geiger and Leslie Davis, "A Growing
    Number of American Teenagers—Particularly
    Girls—Are Facing Depression," Pew Research
    Center, July 12, 2019, https://www.pewresearch
    .org/fact-tank/2019/07/12/a-growing-number
    -of-american-teenagers-particularly-girls-are
    -facing-depression/.

18. Katie Young, "3 Ways Gen Z and Millennials
    Use Social Media Differently," GWI, April 5,
    2018, https://blog.gwi.com/trends/3-ways
    -gen-z-millennials-use-social-media
    -differently/.

19. Wiedmaier, "Gen Z, Identity, and Brand."

20. Ramic et al., "900 Voices from Gen Z."

21. Wiedmaier, "Gen Z, Identity, and Brand."

22. Tim Keller, "Our Identity: The Christian Alternative to Late Modernity's Story," Wheaton College, YouTube, video, 36:45, November 11, 2015, https://www.youtube.com/watch?v=Ehw87PqTwKw.

23. Matthew 3:17, NKJV

24. "Tim Keller on How to Bring the Gospel to Post-Christian America," The Carey Nieuwhof Leadership Podcast, YouTube, video, 1:07:56, May 12, 2020, https://www.youtube.com/watch?v=zNve3Hexh28.

25. Tim Keller with Kathy Keller, *The Meaning of Marriage: Facing the Complexities of Commitment with the Wisdom of God* (New York: Riverhead Books, 2011), 44.

26. 1 Corinthians 12:12-31

27. C. S. Lewis, *Mere Christianity* (New York: HarperOne, 2001), 133.

28. John Calvin, *Institutes of the Christian Religion*, trans. Henry Beveridge, ed. Anthony Uyl (Ontario, Canada: Devoted, 2016), 18.

29. Peter Scazzero, *Emotionally Healthy Spirituality*, updated edition (Grand Rapids, MI: Zondervan, 2017).

30. "The Johari Window Model," Communication Theory, accessed May 31, 2022, https://www .communicationtheory.org/the-johari-window -model/.

31. Jeff Fromm, "The Influence of Identity: What Gen Z Wants from the Beauty Industry," Millennial Marketing, accessed May 31, 2022, https://millennialmarketing.com/2018/01 /the-influence-of-identity-what-gen-z-wants -from-the-beauty-industry/.

32. Tom McLaughlin, "Expert Offers Tips to Help Teens Deal with Social Media–Related Stress This Holiday Season," *Rutgers-Camden News Now*, accessed May 31, 2022, https://news .camden.rutgers.edu/2019/12/expert-offers -tips-to-help-teens-deal-with-social-media -related-stress-this-holiday-season/.

33. "How Do I Study the Bible? Grace Church Position Papers," Grace Church, accessed May 30, 2022, https://gracechurchsc.org /wp-content/uploads/2011/03/15_studythe bible.pdf.

34. "Lives Transforming Worksheet," Lives Transforming, 2009, https://drive.google .com/file/d/0B4bYNMXHy4PpY2dURHlh MnRPc1k/view?resourcekey=0-g-v -leMm6en0Pxb3BaWEjA.

35. Jenny Anderson, "Why Are Our Kids So Miserable?" Quartz, March 21, 2016, https:// qz.com/642351/is-the-way-we-parent -causing-a-mental-health-crisis-in-our-kids/.

36. Stanley Hauerwas, *Sanctify Them in the Truth: Holiness Exemplified* (New York: Bloomsbury T&T Clark, 2016), 85.

37. John 13:23

38. Mike Jantzen, "Is Jesus Really Ok with Self-Love?" The Life, November 2019, https:// thelife.com/go-love-yourself.

39. Romans 8:17

40. 2 Corinthians 5:21

41. Psalm 139

42. See 1 John 2:17, NLT.

PARENT GUIDES TO SOCIAL MEDIA
BY AXIS

It's common to feel lost in your teen's world. Let these be your go-to guides on social media, how it affects your teen, and how to begin an ongoing conversation about faith that matters.

BUNDLE THESE 5 BOOKS AND SAVE

DISCOVER MORE PARENT GUIDES, VIDEOS, AND AUDIOS AT AXIS.ORG

ax̆is
www.axis.org

CP1805

PARENT GUIDES TO FINDING TRUE IDENTITY
BY AXIS

When culture is constantly pulling teens away from Christian values, let these five parent guides spark an ongoing conversation about finding your true identity in Christ.

TEEN IDENTITY

LGBTQ+ & YOUR TEEN

BODY POSITIVITY

EATING DISORDERS

FEAR & WORRY

PARENT GUIDES TO FINDING TRUE IDENTITY

BUNDLE THESE 5 BOOKS AND SAVE